Piec[illegible]
Of You

Calum Cumming

chimpmunkapublishing
the mental health publisher

Published by

Chipmunkapublishing

United Kingdom

http://www.chipmunkapublishing.com

ISBN 978-1-78382-260-7

About Chipmunkapublishing

Mental health books give a voice to writers with mental illness around the world. At Chipmunkapublishing we raise awareness of mental health and the stigma surrounding mental health problems by encouraging society to listen. We are documenting mental health literature as a genre so history does not forget the survivors and carers of people with mental illness and disabilities.

To my late parents Norman and Betsy

FUNERAL OF A SCOTSMAN

Gisela looked gaunt as she stood in the shrouded swirl
With Anna her blonde daughter some way from the men
I glanced at their winter illness as I carried in the casket
To the tan sandy freshly cut grave some six feet deep
The ground was broken Braigh wall by shovel and Lewis brawn
And yet I still looked and hoped to see my mother
Yet I saw Elizabeth and her beautiful specific Skye Ross cousin
I was at the head of the coffin the business end
The thick end of a short life: some 69 years
The coffin would not lower in the hole
Dougal told me to go right to the end
And the panic was over finally
The service was read and then we all shovelled in the fragile grave
For it was the Lewis way to stop things falling apart-Eden game
To cover up the body after Robin had cast-some brother: he was startled
At his own sense of mortality for Robin was a modest man who inhabited the twilight

So the pipes began "The flowers of the forest are all weeded away"
He was a Scottish Prince Norman and the head of Comraile Nan Eilean was there.
There had been the exact wreaths of flowers on the coffin but Mackenzie's stayed
Wrapped. It had nagged at me it still does that cellophane Calum, lain and Stuart
For Norman had been careless with wife and children and lain had taken the foot
It had been dark and dank and we stood in a new bright beautiful place
As the sun broke out in laughter for the piper had been paid twice
And the guile of the highlands had danced away the notes in his sporran
We took Keneth Maclennan's Bus back to Stornoway to offer hospitality
I sat next to the crofter who pastured his sheep on Norman's 13 acres
He offered up a wedder once a year so he could keep his free Grazing; it was not in
Doubt, for the Islands meant there was not much money
I got off the bus and said to my brother l was going on my own first to a bar
I wanted to be alone with a large whisky a cigarette and my thoughts
I was so selfish I sat at the font well and thought of the money I would be left
I could tap into more and more of the maltlets I thought
And buy a car. I had been poor since 91. Completely Poor
And the ordered cheque had fluttered to the floor as Norman died

The king was dead with his alibi of a faun or Peter Pan
As the barmaid spread the ashes of the colour of a fire
Orange and yellow like the brief sunlight externally
Another battle won both inside and out
For I was cast as the Patron Saint of chaos-St Jude
Even though I was grieving I searched for a meaning
In the licking flames of that coal and peat fire
From Lewis to Los Angeles I had read the poster
At the airport when Iain rejected me passing on to Kenneth
I was hurt but tried to forget the other side of love

PIECES OF YOU

The grey backed mirror shattered on the concrete slabs
But what really mattered was not luck or malice
I was left thinking of you in Soul neon Gemini sea green
Or was it Adrienne, Betsy or Jewel however consciously the crunch of
My boot prints song exposed the laced front face: the repose of Eliza

You like me are Norman in sapience and budded growth
I looked at the scene in my back-cud. bins and the glass
This flat had been my first piece of luck in seven years
I still rue there the bad luck mirror of my neighbours
Who I thought were happy with their children
But like a contagious disease suffered the malice of Scots
But sadly for I loved them they are replaced with a cripple
And her bastard tribe who phone for the police
When I search for answers in my muse

Keep the village alive I say not dying washed up
On the shores of a brisk Edinburgh beach
For as I see the cripple and her 20 years younger man
I realize that in their case love is a birthright
And I realise once more I will have to get out
If I am not to be turned into the village idiot

ERNIE JACK

I knew you in my Wimpey days
Foreman Brick layer sage
We would pour over the drawings
You turned arguments into knowledge
So bright and intelligent
A dusty summer sparrow. a noble winter hawk
So good at your blue/grey courses strength
Making storey roads and cement cubes
That we had hatched together

I only knew that you were a master mason
For you were never on the tools and tingle
Sorting booted and catnic lintels and frog up
Checking bitumen and UPVC damp courses
Setting out stepped lead flashing, and supervising
You would take out your glasses from the case
Stand on your soles and watch me find the right way

On a Friday you would get happed with vodka
For Ernie you could not hold your drink
But like the rest of us it proved an antidote
As you badmouthed salaried staff in Lamb's office
I earned a fraction of your wage and I would take it silently
For you were another man that led me into the light
You were from Arbroath-that declaration of manhood
A map for the true horror that granted us an Empire
I often think about you and your classical British homes

You are dead now some twenty years of powdered aggregate
Jack is the Portland cement and earnest is the bagged lime- I: 6
That flickers in summer working amongst the Benford
The quiet Aberdeen Angus Leo led by the picked water
Towards the black dog bar in winter blizzard ghast
For a hot bar lunch with the young girls Jill and Lisa
Elisa my sea bond of planted love

THE WEST END HOTEL

I sat on the wooden Kist beside Jack
My Clarks leather sandal dangling one foot
It was my second coke: how nice
I suddenly spoke to Jack
Who was reading the hot spur?
"Will Dada be long?"
"Shut up and drink your coke"

The hotel was busy in there
What did they do at night?
Sylvester came by and I stroked him
There was voices and music
Coming off the back of the full studded door
There was a constant hum and the smell of neon
Coming from the half open black halved bar door
Dada came out with Enoch and went into the cramped toilet
The loud metallic riddle was coming out of the door
A taxi I noticed had appeared at the front door
I heard Dada say as he spoke to the man in their kilts
"Him in there is one of those chaps that sit down to piddle Ha"
Down by my feet there before us was a puddle
For I had spilled my coke Hooray it's time to go!
Jack had joined the men for a pee and the taxi naturally was for us
Soon the gas of Red bank, bed, Mama and Garrulous food
For I had noticed on the Mum's train journey to Edinburgh from Aberdeen
The white-disked aisle lights
The coal at Hay market the double 0 7, Friday at the top of the hotel
On Prince's street rubbed a spitted tissue to my face
For it was summer the time of easy friendships and I was five now
A world of toy guns for I learnt to cycle at six or maybe 7?

If I had known then as the taxi door closed on that place
How life was brilliant why I far sooner than now
More admirable than cold spring Aberdeen rain
Would have been less damaged by bi-polarity
Jewish Celtic west coast warmth
Of the non Indo European micro family

REALITY

I am a little man
My father said to me
"I don't suppose you will ever amount to much"
It appears he was right
For I am almost 53 and have nothing
I don't have a job and haven't had a girlfriend for 23 years
23 long lonely years suicide attempts, schizoid tendencies and Bi-polar
Who is going to look at me? With my alcoholism and self-pity
I have no children and no wife
I get so low sometimes for I am a failure
Finish

In our own country and seeing the barroom
The jukebox played The Shamen Love Sex Intelligence
"Stand by your beds hands off cocks on socks"
I shouted for I was a little SAD
Doug had a whimsical smile on his lips
As I fought mania at the bar and imitated a stick down
For Doug like me had realized they were children
Up here in the land of Anne and Gus

I had just done a day's hard work
It was Cocktails after the water board
Where I had spent the day in Deeside
It was early hot summer May 7 a Thursday
I had seen Guy by the Invercannie works
Ace key as the Archimedes lift pump screw
Standing by the roar of the mesh net boundary marker
Like the claw marked gangster and his face was open
For he understood water for Madonna was running soul
All water, plant, fecundity has the bawl of the dog's run
Superior had let him in the deep truth of it's yellow
She was a lovely girl that went around like a ray of sunshine
Guy was the antidote to Year's strangeness-for he had said-
To doctor the reservoir with LSD
Fast cars, French, good food and beautiful women
For Guy understood as a Ritchie that Aberdeen was strange
The canker that dwelt like bain, the gothic weirdness
The souls that dwelt in quitted silence
For they had grown sick in health
So far away from civilisation
That day like the swirling drink, inside Guy
As he faced me off, the Bruce fought, the Ritchie
Was searching for a wife, for he had learnt from O'Neal
That you had to be the fox at the fowl coop
For he had made the first visit to the chamber
With Madonna Louise…
And now? Well now he stood slight awry but sane
As a Prince can be who needed his goulash
Guy had horse-powered after I saw the Vic in his tanned face
To Aberdeen and Jackie Sinclair in the Covenanter's
The plumber and keeper of imprisoned souls

SUPERSTAR

She woke at eight-fifty two
And put on her make up
On top of a cleanser face
That had re-hydrated

She was tired
From her LA concert
She lit up a rare tip
Looked in her dead mother's mirror
A country Canadian & French peasant girl

Madonna from Naples keeled a little
For, come on, she had been brave
The photo of Don Juan peeled cornerwise
The little dark Spanish blue eyed matador
Famous for his peace loving nature
Rum & raisin in a Four Bells raffia box

She had travelled the fates
To realize that she was
The bled heart of the superstar
To burn like Mount Etna-silver and gold
So in truth there was nothing but sob and ire
In her beautiful sensitive season's green eyes

She sang a song as she looked in the mirror
Good to see you again...
Love had broken her heart
But yet as the cell phone rang once more
She turned it off and thought of Guy:

Drummond's bar Aberdeen sinister 93'
As the Black Douglas broke rancid

I had seen him once I thought
God he was like a hurricane
You could have been anyone to me
As you smiled at me
Madonna Louise, her season's royal flush
Her true love was Guy for she has 40 years left
Then some twenty two years ago perhaps more
Like the body of evidence as it seemed then
He is a magnetic Scotsman
A Bruce not afraid of anything

For in a haze of Lambert and Butler
Me looking like Thomas De Quincy
Douglas sitting amongst the girlies

CONT P.5

PHILIP AND ELIZABETH

They have seen so many changes
Oh darlings let's play our hand
Lovers

And yet you seem so young
Lets head in now
First

Free in two houses strength
The sign of change
Hurts

Yet I take the thoughtfulness
Of our two Elders
Now

Mum your true service
To this Potato
Tattoo

Driven now (accept)
German Norman start and
Pride

I reel in now, Je suis Charlie
Lisa wants little
Me

We will no longer part
As I go through this
War

Thinking of your father's strengths
As we get ready for radio bed
Dreams

Mum the night slips away like an eel
I am earthy come on
Darling

Where is mum? Please
For need her calm
Paris

Crack along side
A duty

POLO NECK

She looked like Norma Jean In her red robin polo neck
Black woven Pigtails blue denim hipsters
On the childhood farm, all we have left is photos
And uncertain wavering human memory
Yet the image endures and I am left wondering
If Bob Hope had used cinematography in his nativity
Of East Coast road trips up to see Jim and Bob Gall
Somehow I think he did for I loved Bob Hope

All we have left is Betsy and Sean; that precious human cargo
For Angus like Banffshire is truly magical in the summer
The brave new world of the late 50s' Blue sky heated by yellow sunshine
A fragile thing like old age or the resilience of childhood
To be loved in familial play for with rest, food, work-almost all we have

I drove up the estate tonight and saw a woman cursing and Davey drunk
Is that our lot to be restrained by harsh words or drink?
There is now the money tree to change things-ameliorate Scotland
For Joanie found the pain of what is old and now shabby too much to bear
Yet I talk in the cold of the winter solstice; things will look different come Mar

People are jealous of what they cannot understand or have thought about
So they deface the substance with the crude daub of language
Or perhaps Liza they are just trying to coax this shy man from his shell
Whatever the reason I feel happiest in my flat for now mateliss
Norman and Stuart the phlegm isle polo neck-dirty blonde like New York
I prefer a black poloneck and lain wears red-his patronym
For he is a Comyn of the Buchan
I am younger in years yet I am a little older in DNA as ER discovered
We are both the same though inspired by the Norman Christ Kings
Stewarts-The cream of the barley is a mark of respect more than a Grant piper

Comyn-Bruce-Gaul

The tun of my DNA rings true like a triangle
That should be the paradigm of m) three sexes
The fourth estate can make of it what they will
For they cannot even guard the truth of innocence or experience
For if the bible is right and I am the King of Joab
IT is all mine and you bastards I will make the poor rich
For I have been on roads m) beating heaven constructed
Dug dug crate crate metal metal bitmac bitmac...tar sand
Calum's road to world peace and Jack's also San Simeon
Relative ages of long and singing ringing trees-drench of rain
For 0 is 2015-2000 or 1 TRILLION

The tartans of Scotland France and Ireland wait our turn
United by this sallow and shallow knee deep quagmire
It is easy to say for there is few left to look up to
For we you I must carry the fire after my Dad's sagacity
To be renewed as boom and bust has strengthened the genes
Look from further afar until the truth is you a couple dancing
Abuse, domestic's breakdown
One day John we are teachers for lam Friday's Child
You Monday the-8th day-"a fresh star"
The strength of three leading seamen rowing for our Queen
You draw encouragement from the tide of futile dreams
Your true aspiration is to see once more happy families
Is it dangerous to think or dream of a higher status?
That status devolved of the reasons for violence in Alba
Listen you Hoxa the Commons and Mackenzie are alive in one family
So blunt that kith and choose to live with kin
Or else Kite string will be replaced with barbarosity
Lest we forget, there will be more Korean division bell

Iain James Cumming ascend to what is yours by William's convention
The wild eyed cry out into the night, quell that cry, with equity
For my part my light is only a shy girl, her place is at her Prince's side
For I have reached a state of grace where I do not tolerate striplings
But rather proselytise the cat haters
But come with maximum and watch the pussy willow tree grow in the cool shade
For I like my brother reject the downright trash of most godhead
That is my final line to behave like a Prince and be a loving man
It sounds like you hold your finger in the dyke Jack

KING

There is a gold star Glaswegian
Some may call him Bruce or Cumming
He has the canned juice and I am Iain's brother
For Johnny anything you want is yours
It is your destiny to usurp while I burp beery gas

Born on Monday 17/04/61
First day. first lunar sign ... FIRST
The two souls of lain and me are magical-fire, earth=dust
In conception water and fire
There is but though hanging at the end of a GLZ sentence
For you support Independence whilst the Goethe's whirl
A plan based upon sole survival
But you are first and I am the second son

All Betsy did makes it safe

See wedded Cumming years unfold with snake love
These people in Scotland have mixed views about the EDF run off
The land that has aroused suspicion in the Palace of Westminster
Truth said that is the House of Commons, parliament
To be illogical a bottle of proof malt whisky
For there is to consider another Comines Lilly
Comic and le coq sportif England and Celtic Wales
Our triple proof is electricity
And for your part you have got England in your palm
Leodhas women are an Embassy -like lain
While him not in vain
At a wonderful world

She rising like Aphrodite from the foam
For you are but a loving player in the Common Destiny
Just speak and drive away from all that Jealousy
So I can run amongst the fields of barley

My soul guide is my heart that sees concerned beacons lit on the hilltop
As a staff and guide to our daily wakeful hours; our common journey
The pilgrims progress on the Mayflower to New England
Or to disembark in Ellis Island for processing and assimilation
I will take only what I need from it for I bow to no man
I expect no man to bow to me except lain for he has Majesty and grace
He has his spine intact and orange Protestant
For he holds the cinders of Christina's hot grate
I will be the first to find out if love's flower opens
The Mackenzie Breaks, the Donaldson Murkle
Stuck and pinned to her Butt and vacillation runs through it
By breast and clasp we stand at her moaning rampart

CC

To watch spinning wheels
Spoke
Watch your melons
As the ramp dropped
Smell of oil and petrol
Delicious
Give her some Wellington boot
Kick start her
Lions
Jeans and white tee shirt
Jack came in third
Leo motorcycled to sharps Hamilton
Bin
Because. the night belongs to love
Tubs. adhesive, asphalt
Should have been the C
Sickle
Bad news for Sid Barras
Plough the road
Forge ahead like Diana
Do you believe in life after love?
Bin
Left rusting in the bone yard
Amongst the grease and shit
We were born to be wild
Acid
Bum the road up and down
The owl hoots looking for mice
Hay tied to the nineties
Because Jack is a Nicholson
Mother's

Right black Coming rescue Eliza
Because she is lonely
For there is no doubt
She craves something-a ride in my
Fiat

THE DUKE

The model Zulu Smack Norma is home in Lewis
Being rigged by a master mariner in The Eye Peninsula
To be returned for next spring, by me, for my children
Kate is Pregnant to give birth after this indeterminable winter
So much happiness will come for her and William
The image of the poppy sticks in my head
For my Grandfather Ian survived WWl
He died as J was in Betsy's womb -there was Norman grief
Me a mythical bull twin conceived in Leo
My ascendant moon is in cancer as r smoke
Most creativity is born on the cusp
Strange the pang of the wedding arch
For it is truly archaically Eurythmic
Like ancient mysterious sunlight
The golden Bough of Philip

A personal moment for perfect consumption
Kate's second born in Odyssean form-a totem
A new benchmark for your young family
For the blood is strong the heart is highland
It will be their last child I think
For they would like to live a little
Only unguarded revelation
Could deny the Windsor legends
Kate-such a civilised beautiful woman
William is blessed with her confidence
To treat her as his 'Thoroughly Modern Millicent

Charles Street in Aberdeen
Once home of Brown Root Wimpey
Still he waits to take rebirth like Nigg
For he is a sensitive man who does not act flash
But waits like the Zulu drifter to take to the water
Bite into the wind like a born black natural
Instead of repeating long repeated lines
I can only imagine his premiership
A penny for your thoughts Charles
For I know that I must say thank you
I thank you here Chae
The dedication quartet
Of Philip. Elizabeth, Charles and Camilla

FREEBURGER (P. 14)
CONT,

she would be back in twenty minutes. The signals turned green and they crossed into the rimy cold of the city front.

FREEBURGER

Jack was in washing some dirty clothes
His time in the busy city had come to an end
Thankfully (For he was poor)
And his short marriage was over

She was the most attractive woman
That he had ever seen-
Burnished
Jack was too shy to speak

He looked at her in her blue hugging jeans
And he realised that he would miss USA
Tonight was his last night for bad liquorice

'Baby don't cry ... He stammered at last as he spoke over
Clothes she was taking out of the spinner-
She smiled and said 'Never mind your game of Roulette
'Don't fall into the swirl he said and he noticed from her gold watch
She was rich as (what) he had been before she had come to Portland from Texas
'My name is Gill,' she held out a reddened hand gently and said
'Would you like a free burger Jack?'
'Because I like their taste I have been waiting on you'
'Here lets get the dog over- my address and phone number Jack
Jack glanced at the number
She lived in the Ventura near LA.
'I write plays, she said, comedies
She slammed the lid of the spinner
'How about a meal?
Jack's clothes were on wash, it was started, he would have about 20 minutes to go into Subway for a burger. The Laundromat, Cleaneasy and Starch' was an easy walk on the crossroads with Belmont and Main-North West-Portland Maine. Where the little black children squirted and darted back and forth. He looked at the telegraph pole diagonally across from the Laundromat once more. He saw the black plastic insulated lazy bending cables going in every junction and way and wondered how it all held together-I mean it all worked and was responsible for telephone communication-as the crows flies from that brown creosote Douglas Fir telegraph pole. It seemed fragile to him somehow-for although he did not know it he was fragile also. The burgher. He was at the end of his time here and he was standing at the crossroads with an important choice to be made. Was his future guaranteed or would he now embark on a road of despair and toil-because foolishly he had invested everything in a marriage that had turned out to be ugly and loveless "C'mon," said Gill, looking like a doctor at the early dusk of the early March suppertime. "Lets go for a burger." A fire burnt in Jack's loins. After Macleod had left her navy blue skyeways holdall with a basket of jumbled Tee shirts and underwear at the counter with the Little Filipino worker. She had given her ten dollars to pack the bag and said

Robert went into Stephen Loves Tobacconists on Gerrard Street. He had seen the silver Ronson lighter in the window a month ago-and so today was Valentine Day. He had decided to buy it for Baba. He opened the glass and wooden door and walked in through. Stephen was on the counter wearing a grey nylon frock coat and shirt and tie. He was bearded, balding about 55. Robert said to him, "Hello there I am wanting a 28 gram packet of Dumas tobacco and two packets of Rizla blues please." Stephen replied, "Certainly sir," He went to get the tobacco from the many multicoloured ice ribboned cream cool Tobaccos and domestic blend cigarettes that stood behind him. As Stephen went to get the Dumas rolling tobacco Robert looked at the Cuban and American cigar's that lay in the front of the waist high glass display counter. In there was King Edward Imperials, Monte Cristo cigars and Romeo Y Julieta cigars as well as Henri Wintermans half Coronas. Stephen smelt the wonderful citrus and burnt walnut of the many pipe tobaccos in the candy Jars that stood against the back cabinet. He lit a filter blue regal from the ten he had in his Levi Jacket and inhaled deeply. There was an ashtray on the counter that Stephen emptied and cleaned after each customer had made his purchase and left. It was Friday the 14th February 2009.

Stephen said at his back "It's a nice day sir-a day for being outside." Robert looked up from the cigars and replied idly, "A bit chilly but at least the sun is out." Robert started coughing wildly-retching and Stephen turned and said that's a nasty cough you have sir, would you like a sip of water?" "Robert spat some phlegm into the spittoon and Stephen repeated "Just a little sip of water sir." He poured a small glassful from the iced replenished glass jug he kept on the counter. Robert took a sip and said "Yes that's better." Stephen said, "There's your tobacco sir is there anything else 1 can help you with or will that be all?" Robert replied, "I'm interested in that silver Ronson cigarette lighter in the window, can I have a look at it please?" Stephen put on his glasses and said certainly sir-he went to fetch the lighter from the window display. Stephen stubbed out his Regal filter in the grey gun metal ashtray. He noticed that the ashtray had been fashioned from the base of an artillery shell.

Stephen produced the block oblong ribbed silver lighter and laid it on the glass counter. From under the counter he brought some Swan flints and lighter gas. He expertly put in the flint and filled the lighter with gas. It was a flip top and the little striking wheel turned sideways. In an instant there was a flash or two and the lighter ignited. Stephen indicated how the gas went up or down with a small lever situated in front of the burner. At full tilt the lighter was a veritable flame-thrower and Robert was duly impressed. Stephen said, "Here sir you try," and he handed the block lighter to Robert to try it out. Robert held it in his palm. It was heavy and Robert felt sure that Lisa would not lose this one as she had lost her bright metal Zippo some 9 months ago.

THE CINAMMON GIRL

<u>A simple but deep tarn of truth wrought from honesty</u>
Breasts as sweet and delicious as melon
The South East French civet heart of gold
I had been looking for a girl who had lost
Tobacco once or twice

She had never told anyone what lay in her heart
Lisa felt that she was now Ready for him
She really loved her cat and the poet Robert
She had surrounded herself with people that
He would love as baba had loved Francoise Sagan
The drying fishing nets outspread in the sun

It was empathetic how C Boy would talk of sin
The art lovers that formed unoriginality in faith
For C Robert had moved on from that eye book
She was scared of C Robert's searing truth him
Loving her

Lisa was apace her head looked like Robert's
They aware of the same stable a long time ago
It was hard that he was a Scottish Prince-soul
That hated the cheap dialogue of his character
For there was no original sin with soul-mates
And their common seed had left strong genes
Normandy

The aftermath of that had been sore overlooked
He had a history Robert of uncommon selfishness
Of his lack of humanities in those skilled in life
Lisa spoke unlike fat wasters like Rusty Trawler
Lisa just wanted to be alone with a new rationale
Instead of this; intangible harvest of barley alcoholics
Hap does not thank the squawking Pampas beast
Means natural Death

So Robert what of that past un-poetic cat ghost grey
He was a feline George the greatest faithless bastard
Who like the French family had left Aberdeen's gene
Class easy and bright eyes tall with good white teeth
America has come over to Europe to Calumet Robert
He had sacrificed Cumming to C for his USA fan base
The black threshing swell that sucked mineral passion
After AB25 3SR

Who had a wick in his oil stank
Jack James Mackenzie Comyn
Who cried and cried when his father died
But yet he looked after her affairs
He was a gentleman
His work
That was stuck behind a crush cone
For she could no longer wait to die
But was afraid of the final painful yank

For Colum's madness had whittled her
To a hollow core of seedless cone husk
That, held in the palm, would scatter on the wind
She looked at him with delight for she did not have to survive
She held the two pips of the Braeburn she had eaten
Then flung them awry

OLD AGE

Bridged grey blue eyes
Looked at the photos spread on glass
Yes, the start of the day at 11.52PM
She had resisted mail, the wrack
Kept fit and saved money
Ahead lay the day
It, more, she saw the starring role
As the spider spun a web
She realised that she valued the golden quarter
A new start for a new year

It was easier for birds back then
Life wasn't a closed mind
Imagining her child hand in her father's stubbly dreel
It was an encouraging start-his conduct
He had recorded a hard earned Grieve existence
It followed on that at first light she
Would still be with us
Her loved ones looked at her
She was not on her own here
Betsy the birth moonstone aggregate
Thought they conformed to type

Had mostly. looking at things, rejected her?
She had made a mistake on her Ballot paper
Betsy had meant to say yes but was hoarse
Her delicate Gemini French Scots Gaul throat
She forged ahead courageously
God cracked his cheeks and the wind bustled
Amongst the sham and fire of the light
There would be no male tonight
But the graces instilled in her
Sensitive tigress teacher's hands
Another Lisa child as she hoped

By Jove Joan Gunn! the Sutherland woman
Her carer who worried about her shores
With her ravelled up mind Betsy,
The cared, Colum · s mum, had no pith left
What would happen with antrin now?

And lain classical and round
Who bonded her other Norman Weir Of Hermiston?
John had always worn The Red Comyn
A political giant of kidnapped minds

2

Left in a cold flat with the brother
Looking out at rain and snow in grey Aberdeen
The colour of the come that contends the egg
For the way forward contains the Kist on the peat moor

A lovely Sunday lunch
I can physically turn back other
It is possible by me going forward
To go back rushing into the past

A physical journey of body and sense
Moves in a complete circle
So there is no choice only fate

Whether to return or go on
Yet we are left with a decision
To return is migratory
To escape unpleasant other
To return to eat more

To go behind or create

I love you Lisa
For as a whole we are clan
Until now to tolerate mainly alone like Oedipus
Until he mates with his care for

As a result of the decision he made
In the round oval world
For how was he to know that
The serenity of together was back home
It was merely a journey set out for him

The nature of the traveller is undecided
That traveller

The road of life is not straight
My chance encounter kissing her
And would have made love
For I was led by genitals sensuality
But that certainty did occur in pain
The laws of procreation that Oedipus broke back
When he patronised his own mother
For only the tooth is left found in the sand

For after the small loves-the licentious behaviour
That is only teenage wasteland
In adulthood as a whole man plus a whole woman
Close at hand is no more than one abiding relationship
And that constitutes many truly happy weddings

The Friday child, mother and father
Living together careful of one another
Until the father and mother leaves the hut
Like me Oedipus the King

THE CHIMERA

You exist in the subconscious mind
Of dreams and hybrid beings
But yeti you scare me

For it is not the Lion's head
But the brain of me
A tiger

Imagination-carved wakeful dead
For it is monstrously difficult
To be button bright

The torso of a lusty yak
A satyr that in most
Has little libido

And body is capable of love
As clocks tick forward or back
For nothing exists in constant stasis
Except universal truths like love

Welcome back to Mr. Sartre's France
So there is the 3rd segment
The tail of the coaxed out stiff penis

Male brain, Body, Sense
The eternal triangle of Thebes
Only three masked actors
Classical choices

Common sense, cereal love

We have travelled
Down the road
And are faced at the fork
With three necessary choices
If we are not to quiver and die
Whether to turn back
Or to go on left or right
The water and light's abundance
Of Venus. for morning star
Mannish and female genitalia
For they say the female mates for life
While the man punches her
Or sexually molests girls

The evening Star

LADY

You came into my life in Gartly
I caught you licking the butter
With your sugar pink tongue and nose
And so you took to my bed tinker cat

Betsy bought a house for you
In Portsoy and I fed you
Raw beef

You could
Not eat anything but the best
With your snowy bum
That smelt of nothing

You slept and slept
On your cushion
By the radiator
As I wrote
My book Commons
You were my muse

You were black and white
And wore a mask
That never slipped
Not once Lazy Comyn
My little Leo owl

You had a family at last
Everything you had
Always craved

You tattooed my stomach
With your cluiks
And when at the end
You died
So bravely
We were all sad
For a long time
For your unconditional love
Had taught us all
How little we
Were

'The Houses are a joint financial venture between The Bank of Credit and Commercial International and the European Development fund," said Jack, Cally Ally is the developer but all he has paid for is the precontract and planning and BoQs' said Jack. Sean sipped on his coffee, bit into a caramel log and suddenly thought about Tiumpean Head lighthouse. It had been built by one of the Louis Stevensons and was 3" off the level. Something was skewed and not constant like the navigation light that shone into the atlantic off the Butt of Lewis. He said "Who are the houses for, I mean I understood they were private houses built on Spec. for the incoming Americans, Dutch, Italians and Germans?" 'They are for Lewis families," said Ian as he corrected Sean.

Nora, a Scorpion, and his Mother's father had been an Aries the first son

Sean was part of a familial unit of three. He was close to his mother Betsy in Leverburgh, in Harris-his elder brother Warren was Aries; the first sign of the zodiac. The rain started now as he knocked and went into Jack's house. Jack was sitting at the table with his laptop open. He was looking at an article about Buffaloes and he said "Hello Sean Boy, comrahaile?" "Not bad Jack are you watching a programme about the East then?" "Just tapping into my Asian travels Sean-they are interesting animals and are considered sacred in parts of the east." "You find them in South Africa and North America too don't you?" said Sean. "Yes that's right" said Jack. Sean sat down and idly looked at the great horned craturs. Jack said, "They form a year in the Chinese calender-the year of the buffalo-and as you know Sean I am a water buffalo by birth." "You are a horny old devil then" said Sean. Jack let out a laugh and went to sway himself a cigarette from the packet he kept in his smart box. Sean lit a cigarette and marvelled at Jack's smart box-it was like a diamond mine and sat by the phone. The scanner was on and Jack said the ship movements were steady today in the Hebridean waters. Sailing between Uig and Tarbert a young woman had been lost on yesterday's ferry-they had found her bike in Uig. It had been a foul Hebridean day yesterday although in concrete terms the news had still come as a shock-for it was August. Sean wondered to himself and thought perhaps someone had put a hex on her and she had jumped. In the Minch in that weather she didn't even stand a chance. The news depressed both men momentarily although it was the pitiless Lewis way that you had to accept bad news stoically. It was true to say though that someone somewhere had had an uncomfortable night. Nancy came into the kitchen and said "Hello Sean" she was terribly deaf and wore two hearing aids that whistled. She was 93. It was time to catch up on his news over a cup of tea. Nancy and Jack's courtship had been truly awe inspiring, for he had been Marine Superintendent in Calcutta during the war where she had served in The Mother Theresa hospital as an ambulance nurse. They had met at a Colonial Service tea dance and as both were from the Islands it had been love at first sight. The horseshoe had been truly forged on the anvil. She was a beautiful woman and with her help the flag of victory was soon in Queen Mary's arms.

The clock chimed 6 and it was time for getting on with the new houses. In a tic Nancy turned from the percolator where she had been brewing coffee and the cake and sweet confectionary. She said, "Mark my words young Sean that car will skid off the road and crash. Like, as you know the only time I have driven a car, My Father Norman's. It was a black model T ford." "Why do you say that Nancy?" replied Sean. "It is something strange in the contract-The houses are being built for Cally Ally Nicholson (Councillor) from Borve in Skye." Said Jack as he left what was left of his extinguished roll up on the side of the ashtray. "Skye man fly man" said Nancy as she muttered an oath in gaelic under her breath. "I'm going to phone Dennis Macritchie tomorrow on Bay street in the paint shop to see if I can get some more news about the houses" said Jack. "Is Dennis still living!" Said Sean; last I heard he was found like a starched piece of cardboard. A stray white cat drunk and incapable in front of his home in Plasterfield. "Nancy came over with coffee and said, "I don't really think Dennis is going to come up with very much." Jack said, "C'mon Nancy whose side are you on."

SKIE

The old man and wife sat
He went to the back door and saw the truth
They were by definition good
Nancy & Jack Campbell
7 Portvoller, Lewis
Houses were being built
By Michael Tyson of Inverness
They were a busy clean contractor
And had built the new "Auld Nick" in Stornoway
They were setting out more founds
And 8 bad been poured bard crate
The engineer worked at the total station EDM
One compass point NE to set out the entire site of 12 houses

He bad on a rucksack and Sean guffawed
For the engineer kept it there-his calculator and field books
It was his sporran
Sean was tired for he was from the culture
It was normal to take a rest at this time
For be had been working since 6
How would he accept the incomers on the Mhor
Compete with their solemn promise?
Yet it bad come as a shock to Sean
How much the Islands had changed
In such a short time
He was 89
Sean was almost 53

Sean stood after knocking before he went in
He caught the light in the sky

It was a rain swollen black in the North-like Ruth's eyes
An abundance of heart broken unhappiness
In the South he saw the coming night of dark brewing purple
It was overwhelming and crossed into the black grey of the North
It was a still night and the heavens communicated themselves
Sean did not pass judgement but merely took the omen of the skies
There was nothing in the light wind that never stopped but increased or
Decreased-accorded to death and what was left unknown
Of all his Lewis ancestors The Black bull was the second sign
Like the Tiger-his brother was the first sign and Bison and be the second
Yet more than the dip of the asymmetric western male as it rose from the east
He was the second sign-The Tiger he had been accorded his worth
As was the Scots way and he was the second Cumming
Born on a Friday at 7 minutes to 12 midday
And more both his parents were Tigers
His father born on the 7th day his mother on the 16th June
And his father's father bad been a Leo who bad married a Leodhas woman

TO BE IN LOVE

26

26

Lisa 2

I remember love
That tangleha
Like a forgotten tangential
Where the rainbow arcs

I am mentioned
A drop of ambrosia
Hanging from the stainless spoon
Food for the horny satyrs and fauns

Canned emotions like a cemented glass brick
That stuns me into shy acceptance
Of the heart that can hear a formed song
The salt rolls down my face sometimes

I feel that I am pinch holed
Like that good peg in the clay under my tramp
I have excerpted the crude linger from my lungs
Of Lewis herring and potatoes on a long demented vacation

Companionship like two people in a sea totem
Of acceptance of my own company
O
Not a man that will ever amount to anything
Left with dignity right to the black end

Where I continue to rage at the changing lights
Or perhaps I may catch the blue siren
The shy sister" s of mercy may gift me truth
A gift for MUMA on the beaked stork of dreams
Communicating my plough shares, link and be happy
For what is left is most important
On the noise and pity of the dance floor

The world is at war
As a familial race we have learnt nothing
From the 20th century
A new millennium creates the flame of a new world war
That betrays itself with a biting red blow
Like handled spade
A dead punk hooded crow
T should not be in love
In such a haste
Until the cunts and angry blacks and tan, honkies, rats
Serve before the conscience of Hussein 2nd

For he will PLAY HIS ACE CARD SOON AND IT WILL BE right too

(P29 CONT OF 28 POEM

A pink tee shirt and gold and opal ear studs
To wear
And she asked wee Mary
For a pair of panties
And CC politely went into the kitchen
As Lisa got dressed
For it was June 8th
Although it had already started to ring
In CCs' heart
That he truly loved Elisa
So they all had breakfast
MC LLC and CC
And CC wondered if like MC
LLC loved CC like old souls
For they were smoking Royals
And LLC looked at CC like a cat
And wee Mary started to cry softly
Lisa said for the very first time
"I love you Calum"
And then there was some rain thunder and lightning
And they all sat quietly a little broken
In the summertime on the hill

BY JOVE

She's a desert rose
Said Moses to the Israelites
She's related to Lady Aberdeen
Replied wee Mary
As she picked her nose
Blethering from the open door
On the catty stool

Put her in an apron and get the Kitten working
Cleaning my living room
Shouted CC from the Kitchen
As he made breakfast
For his sister in law and him
Muesli and a boiled egg
If you must know

And then wee Mary came through dressed
All syrupy like
Dripping in darling and factor 7
She sat her arse down
And lit one of CCs fags
They were taking it in turn
To nurse their hangovers

And then a strange thing happened
On the road to the forum
The door rang
And wee Mary let in Lisa
Replete in green and orange Nike trainers
CC shut his mouth

What a body thought CC
But Lisa simply said
I have brought a jar
Of Walmart chicory coffee
For us three scallies
She had a daft amusing look
On her face as she passed the jar to CC

Then she sat down and crossed her legs
Beside her sister in law wee Mary
So CC made Lisa as well some breakfast
And put This Morning on the TV
Lisa was begging wee Mary
Not to go after chow
And CC gave Lisa a white pair of Jeans

SUICIDE

So I tried again today to kill myself
I tried to hang myself
Out with a bang
The light cable snapped
I flapped for a while
Then felt some resolve
That didn't last long

I have sometimes thought of suicide
It started in the North East-48 Albert Street
After that song in MASH
In the bath before bed
On a cold winter Sunday night
I used to lie on my back
And stare at the acid bulb
After a fight with lain

So today I came close
To Death
Like I felt with Ruth Munro
Some twenty-two years ago
Except this time
It is far more serious
As the drug dealers went to jail
Wheelers and dealers
People with no absolution

Their existence is finite
I think
No heaven like Betsy Caird
Runts and Criminals
Who have led me to be keel hauled
Unlike my Granddad Jim Gall
My words are finished now
Because she has behaved like a heroine
I don't know her but she has silenced me now
I shut them all out The Louts

STARTS 2 PAGES ON → (3)

Deere. Like all the country boys Watty wore false teeth and smoked. As he, like Sean's Grandmother Betsy Gall. had had all his own teeth removed as a teenager. He chewed on a Rennie for he like the rest of the Wimpey boys. although they did not show it. lead a stressful existence. He had acid reflux and the rime of the peppermint and chalk was on the sides of his mouth. There, could be found deep acne pits from spots he must have suffered as a teenager. Waiter hated the city of Aberdeen although he liked Sean for he was of the country. Sean had seen Waiter as something of a father figure. For Wattie would give him food and take him on a Friday in his old Green Ford Granada for a chip supper at lunchtime to the Bluebird in the Bridge of Don.

Sean made a note of the concrete they would require and Wattie said "We've got drinks arranged for you in the Bothy on Friday for your leaving do. Auld Joe ill turn out a few potted head sandwiches for you!" Couttsy was having a condor moment and his pipe stuck out of his moustached mouth. Sean was never able to work out how old he was although he wasn't too old to cut the moss in New Pitsligo bog in the summer. Like everything in the North East Coast it was a commercial operation. Sean looked into the gloam of the clear night and saw the moon sharply defined. It was already as bright as a reading lamp.

"You'll get the bowser at 9 am;' said Sean. "I suppose Hilly" s comes first the hungry sod;' said Peter. For George Lawrence was originally from Laurencekirk, in the Mearns . although he lived in New Pitsligo. As it was Peter drove the crew-bus and held the bunker card for derv and petrol. Sean replied . ..For whom the Bell Tolls-The Bell Tolls for Thee:· Both Wattie and Peter Laughed and Wattie said, '·I can still see your name in lights yet Sean!" Sean guffawed and yelped out, "The Hackney Empire! Boys.·· He quickly moved on.

He passed George Fraser the slabber. He had laid a driveway that day and the two slabbed lanes were like lanes leading from the footpath to the house. He said hello and hurried on for the metaphorical sun was now no longer shining, and he still had to phone for concrete to RMC at Harehill. It was a sand and gravel quarry used for bricks and hatching concrete. Which was still partly owned by WIMPEY; it was near Belhelvie some two miles away. RMC a multinational partner by Davidsons, which was partly owned by WIMPEY. They produced common grey bricks-frog up or frog down they were common grey bricks and seeing that the superstructures of the houses were rough casted WIMPEY used them on the site. Sandy who took the orders at RMC was used to some ear piercing phone calls from Foremen on behalf of their contractors at this time of night. With John Fyfe RMC supplied the contracting industry in the North East with concrete.

Dougie Still the kerb-layer would need 3 cube and the house foundations would take 15 cube. Pip and Gordon Prise were pouring a floor slab so they would need 30 Cube tomorrow. They would have a 5.5 metre cubed bowser all morning.

Remember to tell the men to construct the steps properly. For Dave Barclay the area manager from St Andrews had taught him well that risbond joints in the concrete found steps could lead to structural problems once the structure was live loaded. They would be kit houses. Sean had levelled in the pins that morning and had calculated the hypotenuse lengths between the pins, which would ensure accuracy.. The sine value

He walked east with the dipping grey Doric sun doing ifs level best to remain in the horizon. Sean looked at his watch, it was red 4: 11 pm. He had picked up the cheap Casio LCD watch in the market the previous Saturday. He passed Abbey and Dod who had boned and excavated then pinned 100 metres of steel kerb log shutters that day. Maurice Mucklewhite sat in the WIMPEY orange Ruston Bucyrus 150 tracked excavator. Apparently the machine was underpowered and could really have done with a CUM M INS power plant instead of the DAF power plant in the rear engine compartment. However as it was it was the envy of all the other digger drivers on the vast site. It was time for a mews as the work of the day was over and everyone smoked a Regal King size from our own packet. Maurice did not wear a safety helmet and poured the last of his tea from his thermos to enjoy with his cigarette. He looked like an orange Cheshire cat and was a pithy man of little sentiment. He saw things for what they were and did not have time for cleiking.

Sean said "I will order the concrete tonight for your pour tomorrow Dod. 5 cube of 20 Newton Dod. You'll get the Bowser at 8AM."

"Sine you had better make it 8: 30 Sean." replied Dod. "The shutters still need oiled."
"Okay thank you Dod" said Sean . ..There is aye something, .. said Maurice who Jet out a short laugh and Sean looked at the orange freckles on the back of his smoking hand.

If you at that moment had cut all four of them open they would have bled orange. As it was Sean's Mam had been addicted to oranges when she was pregnant with him. In the gathering gloom their gathering was fate.

Dod wore a red boiler suit with the trousers tucked into steel capped Wellingtons. Abbey wore safety boots and a blue boiler suit with a donkey jacket on.

Sean made a note of the concrete required for Dod and continued on his way. He stopped at Peter Courts the ganger and the other ganger Warty Ritchie. They had been saddling pipes today. They had stihl sawed and connected ten pre-cast concrete foul house pipes with cement fondue to the combined foul and surface water concrete 1.5 metre concrete pipe between MH 17 and M H 18 that lay in. They were constructing Manholes tomorrow and would need 3cube of concrete. Peter was a strong man from New Pitsligo and Waiter was from Belhelvie near the Black dog army range at the Bridge of Don.

Sean took their order of concrete for manhole surround. The shutters sat around the two precast deep manholes like clipped condoms. They would need five cube of concrete as they would be pokering the 20 newton concrete until the fat ran out of the overflow plugs. Waiter was 45, eighteen stone and 6" 8'. He was as broad as a farm door. He kept a couple of cows on 20 acres and ploughed crops with his old John

THE ENGINEER -- A STORY

Sean stood against the picked out definition of the granite and lime random rubble wall. The cold watery sun was setting and the quiet, the atmosphere, caught him unawares.

He was a man of 22 and he had just finished his apprenticeship as a Site Engineer. He was caught still and he thought of how he had not taken the duck green dappled gunmetal Hilger Watts 20"' Theodolite down. He would line up the yellow dots on the instrument and put it in the clay spattered metal box. Kevin the chain boy would be waiting for him at the site office at Lousing time.

It was always the same feeling that Sean had at this time of day. It was time for retirement of the day. His yearning for solitude was broken by his need for company. For did he truly know the men? The caste was approaching winter and at the end of that week he would be leaving George WIMPEY to work for Rimmon construction in the Western Isles his Father's heartland. But for Sean although he had a Gaelic name felt at home here amongst the sentiment, the clack clack of the Doric. For Sean had the Doric and spoke no Gaelic. For both coasts ran in his blood.

It was a private housing estate he was working on and he had realised that it would be time for lament amongst the honest strong men. This company was a family and they had all been saddened to hear about the death of Adam Scott the slabber. He had been left broken hearted and now he was in heaven. His stepson was Dennis Nilssen the mass murderer of Muswell Hill in London. Adam had brought him up as his own son in Strichen although Nilssen was of Norwegian descent and had left school with little or no prospects and joined the Army where he trained as a butcher in the abattoirs of the Rhineland and Colchester barracks.

Something had gone wrong and the grim reality was that Dennis Nilssen with a history of quiet Homosexuality had left the army and had worked in the Job Centre in North London. He was a silent loner and something of the queerness of Greig the open charnel house of Ibsen inhabited his schizophrenic souls.

It was a cause celebre at the time. How Nilssen had taken pleasure in cruelly murdering his young lonely gay guests in his flat in Muswell hill. He would butcher their bodies and buried the body parts in the garden until a dyno rod engineer had inspected his blocked drains. Whether he had eaten parts of his victims remains unclear but he had boiled their heads and something bad had inhabited his soul.

Sean had received the news of Nilssen and Adam Scott's subsequent death with an air of querulous resignation for his part. Sean had always realised that potentially evil people were of limited potential and generally there was a high degree of psychopathic tendencies amongst the culture of the North East.

Sean picked up the instrument box and made his way from the house founds he had been setting out on the hill. The houses would be stepped it was so steep. He would

THE PARADOX

I was disgusted with the common Genet behaviour
He dashed him to the floor with a gutting knife
Did you shut the door to the world or should African Americas move to Africa?
And one the younger-Scar face Johnny Third died. (in Aberdeen)

What was Gavin Kemp but a bottle of vodka and a gun?
Sean breached the cunt and was left with "Death in June" playing
He drinks single malt-that is to come, as Kemp lay dying

We know now he is a gentle lad Jimmy Boyle
He showed guts in the swirling prison halls of Scotland
I like him, for he like me loved his mother and wrote her letters

So that precisely is what that Lone Star State praised
In that church of emotional football and wiggle red rooms
But the bubble & squeak was waiting to be eaten at home

So now?
We are left with a paradox
To be gentle and be with our explicit paradigm
Measured out in 2 litres of strong cider and my cigarettes
Everywhere Brick sows as two
It masks the paradox of my life
As John Joseph Nicholson's double

While Lisa is out romancing with "Him" (her husband)
She protests her love for the old Taurus soak Cal
As the bell rings at Lark hall and sweet bird of youth sing

Penelope Cross is Ariadne
To Javier's Theseus
And Robert is the Minotaur
A point of' woven concentric legend
For like her sworled black arched eyebrows
For she is a miraculous underworld cash cow

FOR JUSTINE FRISCHMANN IN OILS

I) Aries-vermilion red into
2) Taurus-frozen blue into
3) Gemini-soul glass neon green
4) Cancer-custard yellow
5) Lea-harvest orange
6) Virgo-verdant green
7) Libra-soil brown
8) Scorpio-tar black
9) Sagittarius-phlegm green into
10) Xmas Capricorn-barley yellow
11) Aquarius-indigo blue
12) Pisces-semen grey

All bounded by the water from the sky and all four growth elements.
I love you platonically as a soon to be close friend

ROBERT

He stands in the kitchen
Robert looks across the city road towards Elisa's be drawn room
He wishes she were with him here

Homemade French onion soup
Followed by Massif Central St. Teresa Franciscan Nuns
A real sense of freedom Jimmy Boyle

A thimbleful (or two) of Powers
As an aperitif-Summer map threads
When Robert shouts at her wall of blank silence
Because of the jealous dullard

She is going to see dear Franciscan tonight
To give supplication to Holy 8 silence
Craig Millar My lucky number
For she now has a headache
Caused by Bobby's almost mid-day howl
How painful that Mike feels pity
For he struggles with Robert's loneliness

Up in the white timber slatted house
He dreams intuit Kiki and a perfect walk

Meanwhile Jack roams on his motorcycle
Searching for Jacqueline
C'est La
Right this time
Reflects Robert at the cannelloni
Jacque ranges on (You can do it)
And He ends up at the Easter Road
Where he imagines Bono with Michael Collins
Drinking the Beamish Porter

You would not want to hit me Robert
I do not seek more pain but merely solace
Like a two bar heater during the cold damp winter months
I will never ever part from exemplary you
For my part there is no insidious resentment
At least for your sake Cocoa!
Just Stellar argon and Tate & Lyles golden syrup

It dawned on him that he was hungry after two hours work
He is a quick healer Malcolm
He had served his time on the intense blue-eyed tide
He chided his apprentice for Scots tardiness
A man of true integrity the song remained the same
"There is a correct time for everything that small truth
That held the ships hungry cat transfixed
A clean female ratter
That he would on occasion stroke

"Balls said Jim
As he nipped his nail on the black plough tackle
It would be bruised tonight he thought
He straiked onwards up ower the how of the sower park
A rake of shale that subverted the bit
His Clydesdales that intuited the raw scent of home
Girdled them into streaming acceptance of their wark

Both Jim and Malcolm were seared with white heat
Both part of the skelter of the gathering storm
That would try the free world of goodness
I will always remember their wisdom
When I knew them as a boy then as a man
The grieve and the engineer
United by honesty and then came integrity
Into this black integrity
Faith

THE BLESSED MEEK

The riddled loam was fallow
One moothfae of tay
His flask and gallantly breid corned beef
Made by the Donald-Caird woman

She had wished him luck
Earlier on that cold foggy Early Marr
In about the clucking of the cock

They had assembled
Some Gat years earlier
Amongst the circle of feeing clowns
A west water loon
She-Gladstone·s lady's maid
Up by Fetter cairn

Malcolm was obsessive
About his bowel actions and Piles
Petroleum jelly and eccentric bearings
Way below the plimsoll line

Almost the cusp of the Clydesdales
Making light of the ochre reel
For their Doric grieve
Cantering fume from their nostrils
Like Aden's Capstans Navy Cut

Malcolm felt the heat on his back
As he swarfed his naked hands cut of grease
His back was straight like the grieve like
In amongst the drive of the boat
A seeping pipe needed adjusting
A bucket of Souse tonsures at his lugs

Jim worked the sour park up by the Hewitt
Jim felt the war at his back
Young Betsy was in her cotter with mama
It was 1939 a chamberlain year
And yet the park offered up hope
Betsy breast-fed her child
Pushing her lass gently towards the sweet nipple
With strong red culminating Doric wonderful fingers

Malcolm broke Tay, bread, butter and bacon with the English

And the policewoman smiled tenderly at me in Lewis
As I was staying in a Policeman's house
I only wish that more people will read my books
As I read other authors
There will be no need for the bang and clatter
On the deaf ear of the clan

I am fatter
I like Jack, his warmth of character
Although I love Jack
It is possible to love
Like who then?
I would have to ruminate
Like a Texan steer over that cuddy
I do know however that I like Liza Cumming
She has been let down by people who did not love me
People like the broken Latino Adrian Bones
For her I love me
I drone on like a bee stung Louisiana Lip

I made a friend in Lewis this time
Iain in Portville that Norse blood
Who will give "Norma" the Zulu drifter smack
A major overhaul for my children to be

Who knows?

He is 77 the same age as Jack
A mere child in the Celtic lifespan
And yet my mum is going
I encountered some East coast fishermen in Lewis
And felt ashamed of them polluting the noble strength

Outside Jack has on his Nicky Tarns

For he is ratting with blue sulphur for Calum
Like Lady he kills them with one hit

Unlike Babe Ruth he does not miss the vermin

Causing unjust suffering to the diamond back

He makes a mental adjustment

For 11 and 11 divided by 4

Equals 5 and ¼ -one over the tier of death

For it is also his, The Western Isles

My friend and mentor

Robert Macleod contains the EE communication

As well as the 00 gauge

Liza Cumming

She is wrapped around my soul like a woven serpent

A living tenacious thing

That has a majesty in Lewis

Merely symbolic like Leo Alec Morrison's star sign

As long as the adder is treated with dignity

It will not harm you

And the diamond black is medicine

For the poor Apache Indian

Fitter and leaner

Black is the night. ..
She is a sweet May green Garden pea
As I stand at the lea keeping a sharp lookout
As she urinates and uses a Kleenex
"For fucks sake" she says
What would the dug say for she is close in her Cooper "S"
I think of Sally the collie rolling in the dung
The gallant smell the first sense of the plump Ginty
So now?
I travel to Lewis on Saturday
On the Leo birthday
Will she have cake?
For eight and eight dived by five
Equals 3.333% or 33
An exact gill pattern

I am so closely born to that sun
I was conceived on 16/08/61
And still I think all the time about Liza
It is the duck hunting season in Lewis
And the silver bars run fat

For there is only one run in Lewis
Which tugs at my heart like a reason
I plead with myself to take a little courage
Now that Billy Connolly put Killeen out of my life

The Dying mute swan
A Kiss and an embrace of necks
Shoot the birds between our shoulder blades
To her heart the he entreated
Water-the key to her sapience

The moss fell Virgo, dappled and washed there
To the finality of the pavement
Where Louise walks in running rage
I search for the pledge of her, yes she
Chirps in sporadically with requiem
At the mass ignorance of my bad luck
Insurance that quells my passionate bloodstream
For she dwells in the underground
The alternate days of twin eggs are ovular
Ferrous oxide the red corpuscle
That soaks ribbed white cotton

Should I liken her opening to a wound?
The colour of me is wrong I know
For her vulva has not collapsed in on itself

Water has no colours except bloom and reflective wet
The sacrament is taken and dribbles
From my end of the road
Tart and tan the colour of Kilt
Eliza my precious cargo of hope

PRIMO LEVI

Nought goes to ought
They had money
Fascists combed for gold fillings

Big Fear as
Puppies in a Hessian sack
Thrown into a black Gaelic sea

So now sixty nine years after liberation
The weary Auschwitz doors were skelfed aginst
The best talent was almost died

Scots Captain Gumming lived to sixty nine
A Sunday open door-Woody I loved my Father
Broken stumbled knee caps on rusty fails

SY Pleurisy and Pneumonia did for him
Paddled black producing no glut
A Scorpio Saturday night

Shoot the may Eye rope
Suddenly up then slowly down
Will I have Leo or tiger coins?

Clusters of purple juice
Play me your harp Jude
Do you have to gait up?

Is my assumption correct
That they like Kennedy
Are sometime bowed Americas exile

Crappy excuse may tumble forth
From engorged Spielberg gun
What can be done?

Such inbred inequality
Exists Scottish daddy
I want a child why can't I have life?

From a foetal seed

Black hand labour
Field of Scotland
Ceres for the people
The other breed
My Kin's old lead

About you Lisa
My only reason
To roar; not cower
Watery twin child
You came leonine

Sally the collie
Never gave birth
Betsy's gift; Flossy
You are a rose Lisa
Sweet in arbour

Common Labour toil
Drops red on the soil
Harnesses the harvest

Let's go boys
To Hairst

In platonic disgust

Join our hands
Make change
A concrete reality

Damn the critics
The clock ticks
A critic

Touch of that area
More than that
A tan field

Bread and whisky
To stop a while
Feeding the world

Ring sing tree
Fractured beggar
Rise up now

Crucifix
The crucible of the lot
Begging for salve

Barren Cumming
Should he grow?
For spawn is low

Hoots man
Parr haddock
Water born inside

Pattern of dance
Under the hot arc
I sing pan

I feel guilt
For my anger
Confusion of languor

Harvest time gold
A rhyme of thought
Fills your womb

Earth
My gnarled Pentecost
Grow up
Straight up

TO LISA

O Lisa
You are patient
Your true radiance

Let us be
A collie dog
I cuddled

Left with smell
And after shave
Opal studs eau

I leave you
For a while
I am nought

I want your baby
For Lady is first
Eggs of the fowl

You are beautiful
Stasis in thyme
You are not mine

Barnacle
In body
A green shoot

To be cut
And white juice
Oozes forth

These scars
This war
Pattern

World service
The pips
The flesh

Hang the democrat
Greasy Nigerian lie
More human sacrilege

Judgement lies dormant
Heaven wells up

For he is a fabulous player who deserves to bag a brace
They are a good side England
Who cannot go all the way?
George the king to be
The little tot looks like his Dad
And in 1964 Martin Luther King had a dream
Like that fine CELTIC Actor Matt Dillon
So we return to Glasgow that troubled apron city
That sees red as it expresses itself around this time
At the Orange Protestant festival
Dissemination and reverse Diaspora will happen
When Elisa the Paisley Buddy is married
For she has put the cork back in the bottle
ELAINE C SMITH'S and ALLY McCoist's
Of the well welder
I tilt at windmills LLC
For I am nothing without you
Just another poor poet
Who wishes he could
Stop smoking and drinking
And learn to live on a budget

For I only love LLC
For Elisa in all alchemy
Can make a fool of anyone
All of the makers-Dunbar. Henryson. Kennedy
Are not just risen but waiting
Talking in beautiful tongues
A palette right of wit and Hero

For I have waited some twenty one years
For you ALONE my little cat and balanced child
I want to smell your bare knees in summer
Brush your saucy lustrous hair
And let you just hold me
As you gently tease and cajole me
Into acceptance of your sapient care

At Bannockburn The COMMONS for England
For Edward against the BRUS
That bad tempered sacrilegious man the BRUS
Who has with his destructive Skean Dhu ruined his rapacity?
Drugs are destroying Scotland from the inside out
All Elizabeth 2 art is food-STEWART
The multiracial people so tolerant and broad minded mostly
Yet I love my country
The Grampians. sight blonde tartan peaks in a tic turned blue
The scent of nature and the city also
The dear green peace of Lennox-town
Which is healing itself
The Otters have come back to Manchester
The Dee and Don are fat with Salmon

Now I can see that I see this Estate I live on
As a refuge-I am luckier than most
My own space, bright sunlight through Macleod
And now? Mary can cry cleansing her soul rain
For that is the Scots paradigm
The glass of beer, in moderation the whisky
Testicular supply water and demand water
A fight for England that little thing
Who is nothing more than a lousy politician?
Louse on your lapel that bum fat when you kill them
For we shall have a dreamers Socialist government
For all McDiarmid was is the vessel that will carry us there

England play Uruguay tonight in the world cup
I expect Wayne Rooney will score
And prove his manager right Joe royal

JESUS

So now you are reborn
As two right handed brothers
It is of no importance that God has come again
As my mortal mothers eggs and my father's seed
The come of man in the savage wilderness
If you are not to be beaten and left frightened

You did not ask to be born a COMMYN
Or perhaps in a short two years now
To be revealed and revealed again
The finest par salmons of SCOTLAND

For I do not duck to mere beastliness
For you Jesus the original sin
Are more imaginative, more passionate
Than any of the begrimed paucity of thieves

The nation is a myriad of Summer Dreams
And soon this mirrored mortal man will
Be united with his double-his wife
To the mare the colt (the young male horse). has achieved rightly so
And then the rest of the scum will soon be
Paired off with your cell mate
Because faith I say to you this time
We entered nobly, two pairs by two pairs
To the clinkered wooden Zulu smack
And I took my rightly place with LISA CUMMING
A wonderful girl who truly loves her gentleman
Me CC Standing to her left on the entrusted deck

For if you now see me hurt
You Americans are no better than us over the ocean here
For you MC, Jack, Mike
Having your moment of oiled Greek glister
And stepping up to the pewter plate
And helping me in my hour of need
For if as you suggest once digested
The bible is perhaps a great deceit
We will beat them together
For in the holy bible
Jesus is coming Jesus is coming!
THE END OF THE BOOK
What is left of our lives is unwritten

For I CC reject all but the outright world children
There are many beautiful girls in this world
Exhibit your kindness to me is a lot of rubbish

++

+

Trying to come in from the country
The Grampians growl under this frost
Of lies and Density of conceit
Ducks buoy under the uncertainty of wave
That draws the goodness from the silt
And leaves star all except flesh
Beuys understood a little of this Sean Connery
As indeed you do-a vast splintered timber double door
But he inhabited post modernity-a soap world in Krefeld
So devoid of critical acclaim it galls my soul
A place that in Beuys' prime was the human abattoir

Do you want that for me Lisa the human abattoir of brown
For I can do little to stop your pecuniary enhancement
You will have your way little one but you had better grow after THAT
Or you will end up a gnarled bitter old tree that produces no CYCLE
Except bitter crab apples in the fallow months of the year
The glitter of mica then Sean Ryder where the cones are found
We gather them up by the West water in the German POW camp
If you want to understand that and let Anya grow you should read Jessie Kesson

The Czech Kafka comes to my mind a world of dreams where
Metamorphosis defies any critical examination for myself I like to conclude with
Madonna that the apple stuck in his back is the wound of life That Gregor runs FROM

Walking down the Lane with my brother the head it is bright cold, hard edged and devoid of any sentiment whatsoever. No art, no originality just my imagination trying to force something quietly from the urban landscape of that Lane in the Rosemount. Yet somehow I fell as though I had made it I suddenly for one of the first times realised a defining moment in my life dumped into that city and still with all my teeth. Aged 6 1968 winter. And that was it that it was so grey, the city I mean.

I found myself at English, science and drama at Mile-End. For I realised that when I was on the stage I could hold children's attention but also make them laugh. 1 had found a refuge.

TO MY LISA

<u>I really hated you SOME OF THE TIME Lisa.</u>
It is perverse that 1 would do that
As me- PRINCE CALUM ROBERT The Second Cumming
Elective Affinity with the SAX COBURG PRINCES
On the mother's side naturally; Pict, on the Scots FATHER'S side-Norman

Once when I left Primary School and was left with hope I went off the bus during the late afternoon early Last day of primary school and I walked with my friends to the car scrap yard. I was careless like one of those immobile embarrassed rusting hulks in the scrap-yard. For the first time in my life I was happy I was twelve coming on thirteen: it was 1974. I was with Seumas and Patrick and some girls, and I felt truly happy. It was sunny and we were scared to go into the scrap-yard because the man had a big dog so we found some scrap lying outside the yard looked at the remains of a fire under the sun in the grass and sat and talked about the end of Primary school and going. I was to never see Patrick Scott again for he wept away after that saying he would always be my friend. I often wonder what happened to him.

I do not want to Lie Lisa but I must tell you something about the time when 13 I had my Wisdom teeth removed. IT was the bad old days of ARI when I lay in my bed with rows of sick old men waiting to find a way out. I was goofy and I had been offered two options. a brace-five years to come-or this big ghastly operation. I chose the latter and placed myself on the rack. Mica granite. Set out light, filtered like a gearbox. The Lodge. Sour grain harvest purchased hard light. The manly per head doled out wards of ARI. Where orange and yellow of Beatty and O'Neal would roam in their Slater's dark wool blue suits-lending weight to a Free Scotland.

Finally they had struck black gold. They had found me. I was a happy child with my blue eyes, curly brown hair, tanned fit growing body and the brown freckle on my left ear lobe. They were interested in me. They visited me late on a Saturday afternoon-Beatty had a beard and O'Neal was interested in the ward it was 1976. I had been struck down with shingles the previous winter and thought I was going to die then. But that was nothing in comparison to what was about to befall me. Beatty had brought the Telegraph and candy for me. O'Neal gave me a nectarine.

They sat either side of my canary blue bed, O'Neal had read my notes at the foot of my bed and looked at me seriously with bright blue chipped eyes.

So the next day in the morning I was in that coarse North East theatre. They knocked me out and pulled my teeth out and sent a shiver down my spine. I was left in agony. For the first time I had had an operation to straighten my teeth. Lisa was in her Mother's womb with her sibling couriering in and I was crying out in pain. They put me in a side room as my cries were disturbing the old men and causing fracas. We could not possibly have had that in the dry (mostly), cut and dry world of the North East. It was then I realised that I hated the North East.

Let our commons meet
You are such a pal

Cal touched her quivery bottom
Which is very sexy
Then he kissed her on the mouth
Then the beloved one
Was lost to him forever

For Washington DC
Had cleaned and painted the division fence

They will be boy and girl
As Jack Nicholson predicted
In a self-fulfilling prophecy
So Calum had also prophesised

That Jack would tarry a while
And fuse Jacqueline Clark as his bride
For Jacque is the most beautiful girl from Dundee
It is the right fit to bust our loneliness Jack
Elle est un beatifique vin sur L'herbe
As beautiful as Lisa
In her older grace
For the old alliance holds true love

Near the Esk water
I am your soul mate Jesus
My field your moist breath Lisa
I was a water officer
A natural resource
I cried out for you
I did not realise it was blood
Heavy times then Jesus
Not now though
Drink from the deep well
Of human kindness
As Jewel taught you
You kissed the amethyst Queen
When she was a virgin
With her budding breasts and sworled pudenda
Shake rattle and roll Madonna
Principles teaches you August
The Madonna is your older sister
Draw closer verily Lisa
Tell me something of your sport
I turn out nicely
I am Hollywood and smoke Turkish
Sipping and playing pinball
That is when Saul turned to Paul
Hold me once more Jesus

It does not go out the torch
It kept you alive those long cold battles
In spite of your loneliness
Caress me Cal delicately
Let our double helixes meet
Do not judge the congregation above
You are amongst the tarn-off sludge!
Push out the rock & roll boat
In my Arthurian pea green moat
Kiss my full crimson ruby lips

Oh Lisa my dove of peace
We have been apart long
That is as Joe Strummer realised
When it all went wrong
My wee blonde lamb
You
With your Norman hair
Born behind the green shutters
Your true love is my plaintive shout
For sweet Calum is no unkempt lout

I realise Jesus you have been touched
By sadness
Be not afraid your peep peeps are in the glade
Born under the sun

From afar
He was an old tar
She wore Cal's purple and black star
And took care of him
Anointed his god head
And his tender brown back
For truly kindness Lisa
Does not lack
She said to Jesus
What ails your kind heart?
I am wicked said he
I have stung like a wasp
Said cooing Lisa with repose
"They eat not ambrosia
For they are the evil ones
Who has left Christ unhinged"
You are beautiful said he
I am Christ's bride said she
I wear white muslin
My hair is garlanded in flowers
With my open almond back
My crossed soul is gold & platinum
My
Do not bow sweet Jesus
Just hold me light

THE TWELVE DISCIPLES

For her, I really love your voice
Mike for his true tough sensitive courage
Like Mac a Cancer and Fire Horse
Bee it now

Golden Honey that I love
It's a complicated affair love
Trying to supplant Lisa with Nina
It rhymes but not quite
I stand on the right
But I'll never vote Tory
I once went to a bar
I was common muck
Bored down with my spittle
I missed the Capstan Raj on
Turn the rusty capstan once
Sailed Leonine Lisa
She used to walk and look
Waiting for her loon
Who could talk and explain
She waited for him
And he did not love for 42 years
But when he came back
Lisa loved Jesus

Who's the Griffon?
Is it Vladimir or not
For his tribe is ancient
He leads the Politburo
And anonymous peoples
The Jihad has no egghead
The question is can that
Loam be ploughed back
Or perhaps Barrack is crow
"You can't beat them"
Mike is it right to fight?
"We must CC ...
If Europe and the pan African world
Is to be the ark
Of Lebanon
There is no Primo Levi now
Mohammed was a cultural writer
Classical Civilisation"

NELSON

A lovely gentle old man
He enjoyed a half of stout
For the Iron in the brew

Iron in his soul
Robin did not break him
Breaking up rocks

Ooh Spud
Feels good to be free
Loves him rain star

Black soul power
Is evangelical
Up there

Atonement
For error of
Imprisonment

Mike Tyson
Error of imprisonment
RSA in Indiana
As they shaved
Stubborn stubble
In the only mirror
At the head

The heavyweights
Mike & Nelson
Nobles of grease
As Troy cackled
On the block
Black on Black
That petrol emotion
Needs Horsepower
Two universities
Black on white
Tell us Mike
For now you
Jailed wrongly
By a Helen Wright
Nelson's Heir
As Madonna predicted
Hold your ear
To the slab
In damp NY

SHE IS COMMON-PAISLEY

YOUR TRUE GAL
WITH WINDSPEED HAIR
WHO STANDS ALONE

ELISA CALUM
ELISA CALUM
AND AGAIN
CALUM ELISA
CALUM ELISA

THE LL BABY-THE HEART THE SOUL
MAKE LOVE YOUR GOAL

SHE LOVES YOU
TRUE LOVE
IF ONLY CAL WOULD SEE

HE HIT ME CAL
HE HIT ME CALUM
HE HIT ME ROBERT
HE HIT ME MACLEOD
HE HIT MY GUMMING
HE HIT MY MACKINTOSH
HE HIT MY MACLEOD
HE STABBED MY GALL

SEAN IS HATE TO THEM
HATES THEM
JIM SEAN JACK

LOVELY LONELY MEN
A PAN DROP CAN
A BARLEY SUGAR
A BUTTER SCOTCH

PUTRID NOSE OP
NORA NONO NANA NINA
NONA
HARD MACKENZIE BAIN
MADONNA
HARD TACK-LING OR COLLEY
SEE I CC IS ONE OF THEM
SEX SAX SAXO SEAC
HARD WELSH BAIN LISA
FLOURESCENT NOSTRILS
POUNDS SHILLINGS AND PENCE
EMBRACE THE PAPE WOMAN
ANDREW CRUICKSHANK (JAIL)
WOMAN CHILD MAN
WOE OR GO, NO NORMAN WOE

FOR MY WIFE

SORRY LISA I LOVE YOU
HATRED TO A WALL
CALL ME CALUM

VAGINA REGINA MUSTY
LISA CUMIN RUNES
REASON FOR HOXA

MOTHER WORRY SMOKING
DRINK PREGNANT ALBA

LISA, LISE PEACE
PEACH AND NORA'S REACH

COMMON NOTTINGHAM
GIRLS BACK BROWN LEGS

KING IAIN JAMES
MACKENZIE CUMMING I

MA CERT LIB SCOT C ENG-THAT'S ME

PRINCESS LISA CUMMING
MA HONS (Oxon) DIP ED

A REAL SWELL GAL
WHO DESERVES MY FAT HEART

I LOVE LISA JACK AND I REALISE SHE HAS BEEN TREATED PRETTY BADLY BY HOLLYWOOD, BUT SO HAVE I.

SHE IS REALLY SENSITIVE CAL

SEX

Time
I am appreciated
In the morn

The disgust
Over other
Greek's skein
Like a burst football

Intimacy shroud
Translucent water
With pears

Translucency
Currency
Oil

Oh my God
Pen
Fear

Dark night
Come
Hilt cunt

Cock bird
Hen bird
Cluck

Suckle suck
Buck
Juice semen

Musky sweat
Ram it then
Fishy smell

Tire air
Caress violently
Hold gently

Bed beach
Reach over
Boraxed cap

Revel
Dive
Surface

LOVE

To be at ease
In another's company
To put the horse in front of the cart
A mother's love

Ancient young Lisa
To make love in meadows
A lover's love

To be protected
In the shard of the hostelry
To motor on Loch Steisevat
A father's love

To be visited
In the bin
With a precious radio
A brother's love

To enjoy a hearty meal
At the keep of Redbank
Hay and a bottle of milk
Grandmothers' love

To be resent out in Angus
To face the hard boys
To earn country hard worn respect
A Grandfather's love

To be the best country schoolboy cyclist
To be a Scots champion
To not be taken under the wing
To learn adult love

To be let down
By the Church
To be a truly redemptive man
To love myself

To make a real friend
To rattle in the closes
And talk the trade
Now I should truly cherish
Jack Nicholson's love

You wont find out
If you never try

HATE

When I was two in Edinburgh
Father smashed me in the face
He gave me a bloody aquiline nose
Like Majorcan Robert Graves

When I was two in the Fife Kingdom
I hit a child on his toddle
I call myself a man?

A Homeric story after that
Western male
Like Jimmy Nail

That is male
Man passes on misery to man
The Gael is not western
Not Indo European

I am Common Scot
Not Indo European
The Jew tinker
You see I-see Common ones
Have Jew under there olive skin

Jesus veered off line
He showed hate one time
To the Jewish money lenders
He whipped them
Hate against believed evil

I think (Canada) Madonna
Hates evil
Would use her boot
To once blood more than this
Jewish French woman
She would boot against perceived fascism
Then hit and hit and hit against

Jack the organ player wants more
Because I hate the idiots
Then he kicked chrome dome
Because of my tinker mum
That is for me to walking boot hard

You are my friends
I love her smell
I redouble I love her smell
What you've never had

Satanic eyes that view the land
But do not bite the hand that fed them
Jack has no fortune in love
He must re-begin
To live again
Like Iran
An example of Common
Ire
Take Care on your side
That is all homophobes must do
As diplomatic wheels turn
In their fall down
What
It elicits is pity in me

The Scots are studs
Lions out

Move on up to your desire
Yet still the poor dog whimpers and shivers
A firework in the night
That wild dog is fire in the night
At such power I lower
As collie goes to bed in her basket

NE man
An open book
Fed by Norman doubt
Damage is done
I say yes to France's divorced mom
A chromium double helix spelt out concretely
Like a plug of tobacco and a drink of whisky
Scraped silvery scale shimmering
Sirloin well hung beef
As you wont
Alec

Are you not wrong?
Heart attacks
Want
All food is purely good
The rubbish we eat
You provide a service
Fat city
A fond ideal
Divorce would ameliorate that meal
Unequal ascendancy
Because we need you
Without you it would be panic
In Bar Lanark
Harry's game
Some name-Elective Goethe

Dozens of Arrests
Armed storm troopers
Hot coals
You have to heal wounds
Back at work
Hot topics
A need for public debate
On the Common Weil

Unashamedly bias
In favour of a free Alba
Reverse the ascendancy
Release the rubber brake block
Forsyth is a good man Jimmy Boyle
He believes in this Scotland
He suffered unlike your suffering
But you killed man to be free
Is that what you all desire?
The deliverance of death

I have a coaxial mind
With Jack Nicholson

2

For supper for which I Annie, I really beg
You really are all the eugenic crew
And what is more my glue governor
Most of them are cancer blue

My subject-a tough bard boozy race
Hollywood is Oedipus Rex
Mostly the dun
I hi Hollywood
You are pitiless grace
Beautiful curves
A show without barriers
The pipes skirl
The Scottish are come
In the colours of the kilt
A smell of blonde wood
Oozing glorious creosote and amber

A mixture of pace and runes
A community of artists
Some good some maniacal
JN CC MTWB RG SC MC
Carved in the tree of cedar
All below the Scat's heart
OF LC

Lisa
The wee bee
The prop aeroplane
The trumpet wee lamb
The girl's a hoot
Whose roots
Grow into the fleece
And Ark Beau

Michelle A beautiful Black woman

Now Scotland must make hay
Or stay married
18/09/2014
It mattered Tie
Unwrap
A jewel

At the foot of the mound
As best it can hurt
Scotland's piety
The abysmal
Sin hit into
Lisa mom

HOLLIES

You sing of love
Hold the white dove
And let her soar
High up the azure sky

You sing of fraternity
Equality changes as we acquire
A history like milk teeth
That can be shed and take
A home and career and wife
Substance like a strong foundation

We have all made mistakes
But as I see myself now
It is not too late to change

I would eat the dove
Show each other eaten mother love
Children breadth and post virginal
I am fully the Coming

You have never left me
Caught up in my excrement and hate
I have tried to touch your kittens
With my scarred mittens

Jack-cal
Our even hatred for
Hitler's right good luck hand

Hunch on through flying snow
Lucky to be alive
This estate is a dive
Upwards out of earshot
I will never doggedly fly
Towards that erect pistol
Or given under the pointed sun

Some twenty years since I knew love
Flicked into the wind like ash
A lonely Christian man
Destroyed under the leaden sky
Or Want rather the bash
As you tend and prune your peaches
And frolic on Pacific beaches

An old bit of bacon, soup and an egg

FOR MY WIFE

SORRY LISA I LOVE
HATRED TO A WALL
CALL ME CALUM

VAGINA REGINA MUSTY
USA CUMIN RUNES
REASON

MOTHER WORRY SMOKING
DRINK PREGNANT ALBA

COMMON NOTIINGHAM
GIRLS BACK BROWN LEGS

KING IAIN JAMES
MACKENZIE GUMMING I

LIB SCOT C ENG

PRINCESS LISA GUMMING
MA HONS DIP ED

A REAL SWELL GAL

I LOVE LISA JACK AND I REALISE SHE HAS BEEN TREATED PRETTY
BADLY BY HOLLYWOOD, BUT SO HAVE I.

(CONT FROM P1)

Now I loved myself for there was no other here
I had worked here amongst the Gaelic and
Dark entangled locks of the Lewis character
For I preferred Harris. although on the bell
Lewis is no place for the weak livered
For it is an offence to refuse a drink
I had liked Ian Morrison-from Lewis to Los Angeles ...
By dunt of the shovel and pick he was an old buddy
I would go soon to the gathering-would I turn her?
For she was a Skye teacher like Malcolm Mackenzie in spirit
Hot blooded as I demurred at my Father's funeral
Although I would have liked cunnilingus in her black sworled
Fishy opening-Eiizabeth took her away early
This stranger must cool her destitute heels

Lightning Source UK Ltd.
Milton Keynes UK
UKOW06f0051290416

273201UK00001B/5/P

9 781783 822607